Vows Woven in Silk

Silk threads tie the silliest dreams,
Promises spun with laughter's beams.
A knot of chaos, a twist of fate,
We'll make some vows, then eat off plates!

Stitched with giggles, soft as lace,
A fabric dance, let's pick up pace.
Forever's bound with quirky flair,
In our own world, with nary a care!

The Fabric of Intrigue

Oh, the layers of our concealed play,
Unravel the threads that lead astray.
Hidden pockets of laughter burst,
In this fabric, we quench our thirst.

A patchwork quilt of cheeky winks,
With every bend, our mischief stinks.
From seams unfurling, new tales rise,
A tapestry made of surprise lies!

Frayed Edges of Yearning

Edges frayed, yet hearts are tight,
Chasing dreams in the moon's soft light.
Worn-out trousers, yet spirits soar,
In our little world, we always explore!

Our laughter echoes through the night,
With snags and bumps, it feels just right.
Through all the rips, our joy survives,
In every fray, our love derives!

Stitching Forbidden Fantasies

In a cupboard, snug and tight,
Hidden dreams take flight at night.
With needle and thread, we dare to sew,
Secrets bubbling, oh how they flow.

A fabric soft, a color bright,
Each stitch a giggle, pure delight.
Creating worlds of laugh and cheer,
Where everything's whimsical, never fear.

Seams of Secret Wishes

Beneath the seams, a tale unfolds,
Of dreams and laughter, fun retold.
With each thread pulled, a wish is spun,
Bringing forth joy and endless fun.

In pockets deep, surprises hide,
Tickling fancies that coincide.
A patchwork of hopes, we stitch and gleam,
Turning everyday moments into a dream.

Loops of Infatuation

Twisting yarn with playful zeal,
A loop of crushes, oh what a deal!
We twirl and swirl with giddy grace,
Each round we take, a silly chase.

In fabric soft, our hearts entwine,
A playful dance, with every line.
Ribbons of laughter tie us tight,
In the tapestry of pure delight.

Fastened Hearts

With buttons large and colors bright,
We fasten hearts, hanging tight.
What a sight, to see them sway,
In pajama parties, come what may!

Each clasp a giggle, each snap a cheer,
Binding laughter, year by year.
Through thick and thin, we're stitched as one,
In the quilt of life, it's all just fun!

Twill of the Heart

A stitch in time, a poked-out eye,
Fabrics whisper secrets, oh my!
Sewing up love with a crooked thread,
Laughing at foolish things we said.

With twine and needles, we dance in place,
Dressed in odd patterns, a comical grace.
The seamstress chuckles at the patchwork spree,
Each loop and twist, pure delight, you see!

Tapestry of Lost Opportunities

Threads of chance weave a tangled tale,
Missed connections like a ship's sail.
I thought I'd button down my fate,
But lost my thread, oh what a date!

Each frayed edge sings of near success,
A quilt of joy and a touch of mess.
Laughter echoes in an awkward loom,
Where dreams are stitched in neon bloom!

Unraveled Threads of Affection

Tangled yarns of love unspool,
Each knot a memory, a silly rule.
Two hearts, a bundle, what a sight,
Rolling in stitches, oh what delight!

A scarf of giggles wrapped around tight,
But wait! Is that a cat in this plight?
Fur and fiber in a playful duel,
Love is wild, and so is this spool!

Looping Around Dreams

In circles we go, like a merry-go-round,
Chasing our thoughts that cannot be found.
Around and around, the yarn gets tight,
Twirling with laughter into the night.

Caught in the fabric of whimsy and fun,
Where days stretch out like a long, silly run.
Each loop's a giggle, a flustered cheer,
In this playground of dreams, we've nothing to fear!

Folds of Enchanted Wishes

In pockets deep, small dreams reside,
A crumpled map where thoughts collide.
Each wrinkle tells a tale of fun,
Like socks with stripes, but missing one.

With paperclips, I chart my goals,
Juggled hopes in tiny shoals.
A paper fortune tells my fate,
Unfolded laughter, just you wait!

Cuffs of Intimacy

Two sleeves stitched up with quirks and chat,
In cozy spaces, we bump and spat.
Your coffee cup, my secret sip,
We laugh out loud, then take a trip.

Our mismatched socks dance to their tune,
While crumbs of joy fall like a boon.
In every fold, a giggle hides,
Together we ride the silly tides.

Pearls of Affection

With safety pins, we patch up fate,
Each awkward moment becomes first-rate.
A necklace made of jellybeans,
Unwrap the joy in silly scenes.

We hold the world with little quirks,
In bursts of laughter, madness lurks.
With plastic forks, we carve a feast,
In this wild ride, we're never ceased.

Hearts Sewn Together

Two patches stitched on hearts so bright,
We twirl around in pure delight.
With threads of gold and silliness,
We dance through life and all its mess.

In mismatched shoes, we take a stroll,
Through fields of dreams that make us whole.
We tug on strings, our laughter sings,
To life's sweet tune, a playful fling!

Emblems of Hidden Affection

In a pocket, a surprise, I find,
A doodle, a wink, a heart entwined.
It's stitched in laughter, a tale to tell,
Where every thread casts a playful spell.

A sock with polka dots, bright and bold,
Whispers secrets that never grow old.
Each little patch, a giggle concealed,
In the fabric of love, all truths revealed.

Adornments of the Heart

A scarf that wraps in colors so bright,
Is a wink in the wind, a flutter in flight.
Its knots like secrets, tied snug and tight,
Leave giggles in shadows, a silly delight.

Bows on lapels, like butterflies dance,
They twirl with laughter, a whimsical chance.
Each glance is a giggle, each twirl a tease,
In the wardrobe of love, we wear what we please.

Whispers in the Weave

A tapestry woven with threads of glee,
Hides chuckles and grins in each stitch I see.
Under the surface, a jovial spree,
Where laughter is tangled, oh what a plea!

A blanket of joy, all crumpled and warm,
Wrapped up in chaos, a casual charm.
Every fray a story, a giggle relayed,
In this fabric of fondness, our quirks are displayed.

Sash of Untamed Yearning

A belt that's elastic, it stretches with flair,
Holds in its grasp all our wildest dare.
With each wiggle and giggle, it knows what's true,
Revealing the mischief that's hidden from view.

Ribbons of hope in a dance of delight,
Sway like the flame on a warm summer night.
Their twists and their twirls, a comical sight,
As we chase our desires, we leap into light.

Closures and Cravings

In pockets deep, they plot and scheme,
A dance of fabric, a whimsical dream.
Giggles burst as zippers whine,
The treasures tucked in are yours and mine.

The snaps are loud, a mischievous jive,
Elusive charms that seem alive.
Each pull and tug, a playful tease,
In this game, there's nothing to seize.

Threads entwined, they can't escape,
Complicated knots that misbehave.
Yet laughter echoes, joy's delight,
In this fashion, our hearts take flight.

With every stitch, we mend our cheer,
Creating joy that's bright and clear.
Who knew fashion could bring such glee?
In closures and cravings, we're all so free.

Tension at the Seams

A shirt too tight, what a sight!
With every bend, it starts a fight.
The buttons gasp, oh what a scene,
When laughter bursts through fabric dreams.

Elastic bands are pulling wide,
While cupcakes hide, our guilty pride.
The seams are frayed, yet we don't care,
Dance like no one's there—oh, beware!

Stitching laughter with every thread,
A wardrobe riot 'til we're fed.
In fashion's grip, we twist and sway,
With silly antics, we laugh away.

Though tension builds and zippers clash,
In this wild joy, we make a splash.
So let it be, this tale of seams,
With teasing whispers and fabric dreams.

Tender Attachments

With snaps and floss, we bind with glee,
Each little piece, a memory.
A clasp that holds a heart so dear,
In fashion's web, we find our cheer.

Ties that bind and loops that hold,
In silly ways, our stories unfold.
Hitch a ride on this whimsied wave,
With laughter echoing in the cave.

A ribbon here, a bow that sways,
We mask our worries in silly ways.
Each tender hug, a gentle hug,
In threads of laughter, we become snug.

So here's to love that's stitched with care,
Through quirky patterns, we boldly dare.
With every pull, our spirits soar,
In tender threads, we want for more.

Hooks of Affection

Oh hook and eye, what playful fate,
You catch my heart—it's just too late.
These curious clasps, they smile and jest,
In a wardrobe dance, we feel so blessed.

The latches leap like froggies bound,
As laughter echoes all around.
In this quirky bonding, we find delight,
With every clasp, our spirits ignite.

Tangled threads and joyful strands,
Fashion's comedy in playful hands.
A missing hook, we laugh and grin,
For every mishap, a new tale begins.

So raise a glass to quirky clips,
Pulled together by tongue-in-cheek quips.
In hooks of warmth, we find connection,
A funny tale, our shared affection.

Anchored in Emotion

In the drawer of dreams, so snug,
Lies a stash of wishes, warm and snug.
They giggle in colors, bright and bold,
Hiding tales of love, yet untold.

With a twist and a spin, they dance around,
In a fabric circle, laughter found.
Each thread a secret, woven tight,
Adding humor to our silly plight.

Stitching joys and woes in the seams,
Crafting curiosities that burst at the beams.
Here they tease, those little charms,
Encouraging us with their playful arms.

Sashed in Longing

A ribbon of hopes in a jumbled heap,
Looks quite silly, yet dreams so deep.
Tangled together, their stories unite,
Wistful laughter in the soft twilight.

They flutter and flounce with giddy flair,
Each tug and pull brings a cheeky glare.
Oh, the mischief in colors so bright,
Creating chaos, a comical sight.

With the twist of a bow, they skip and sway,
Tickling the heart in a winking way.
Adventures await, with little care,
Sashed in longing, life's funny affair.

Unfastened Hearts

Hearts running wild, in a playful race,
No zippers or locks, just a silly face.
They bounce and leap, with giggles so free,
Unfastened by love, just you and me.

A tangle of feelings, they twist and shout,
Spilling out secrets, all in good fun, no doubt.
Each laugh a stitch, a soft little sigh,
In the fabric of moments, we reach for the sky.

With no buttons to hold them, they often stray,
Chasing the flutters that lead them away.
Yet through every stumble, they find their way back,
Unfastened and joyful, keeping on track.

The Fabric of Us

Woven in laughter, a riotous blend,
Of threads and textures, with twists that bend.
Each patch a memory, quirky and bright,
Reminding us always to giggle with delight.

The seams may fray, the colors may clash,
But like a good joke—with a splash and a dash.
In this crazy quilt, we find our own style,
Stitching funny stories, mile after mile.

So let's dance in this tapestry, loose and alive,
Sharing our whims, where our spirits thrive.
Through the stitches and seams, we'll always find,
The humor that binds, in the fabric entwined.

Pleats of Anticipation

In a drawer, treasures align,
Shiny circles, oh so fine.
They wiggle and they jive,
Ready to help outfits thrive.

Each clasp holds a little tale,
Of wild adventures and a sail.
When chaos strikes and skirts fly high,
They land with laughs, oh my, oh my!

A click, a snap, a fitted glance,
They bring to life a risky dance.
Cautious hearts with each embrace,
In the game of style, there's no disgrace.

So here's to each little round friend,
In fabric fun, they surely blend.
With every pulse, fabric in play,
Anticipation leads the way!

Snaps of the Heart

Oh, those little clangs that surprise,
They smartly play like oh-so-joyful spies.
With every pop, a giggle's born,
In fashion's tale, no one's forlorn.

Metal clicks and laughter bloomed,
When dresses twirled, and egos groomed.
A wardrobe's cheer, a flirty spark,
As fabric grins like a cheeky lark.

Trying on a dream too tight,
A snap unleashed a comical fright.
The fabric stretched, and then released,
Infitness won, yet humor increased.

So next time you fasten up tight,
Consider all the joy in sight.
With every snap, a heartbeat sings,
In style, darling, oh the fun it brings!

Velcroed Vulnerabilities

In a world of soft embrace,
Velcro whispers, finds its place.
With hugs so tight, they won't let go,
They catch our dreams, oh don't you know?

Like best friends in a comfy hug,
They pull you close, no need to shrug.
But when it's time to break away,
It's loud and silly, what can I say?

Little kids in rush to play,
While grown-ups fumble, lost in sway.
A tug, a rip, oh what a fuss,
Life's silly moments, just for us.

So velcro up your heart, my dear,
And laugh aloud, let go of fear.
For in the chaos, comfort finds,
The endless giggles that life unwinds!

The Thread of Allure

A line of stitches, straight and sly,
Threads of mischief dancing high.
With colors bright, they tease the eye,
Each twist a wink, oh my, oh my!

Fashion's charm, a playful game,
With hidden quirks, who's to blame?
In every seam, a giggle tucked,
With blushing vibes when we're struck.

When styles collide in fashion's ballet,
Each thread a joke, come out to play.
A tangle here, a knot up there,
We wear our laughter, strip off despair.

So pull that fabric, twist it right,
In this frolic, hearts take flight.
With every spin of thread and lore,
We weave our joy, forevermore!

The Cradle of Cravings

In a drawer, the treasures hide,
A sea of trinkets, old and wide.
Each one whispers, 'Pick me, please!'
As I buckle down on my knees.

Colors clash like cats and dogs,
A shapeshifter's dream of funky frogs.
With every click, my heart does race,
I wonder who designed this space.

Poking fun at all that's lost,
The funky shapes, they come at cost.
For every smile, there's a quirky twist,
In this realm, who could resist?

So I sift and swirl, my heart on fire,
With laughter born from every desire.
These little gems, they drive me wild,
A playful dance, I'm just a child.

Fabric of Hidden Longing

Behind the seams, a riddle lies,
Each piece of cloth a sweet surprise.
Whispers of yarn call out my name,
Entangled here in fabric's game.

I stitch together moments rare,
With silly patterns, how can I care?
Frills and thrills in every fold,
My heart's a quilt, bright tales retold.

A tug, a pull, let laughter flow,
Mixing colors in a perfect show.
These hidden threads, they gently tease,
As I chuckle, feeling the breeze.

Oh what joy, these fabrics bring,
Each swish and swirl, makes my heart sing.
In a world of choice, I'm feeling bold,
Crafting a tale that's yet untold.

Sewing the Seeds of Desire

With needle and thread, I plot my fate,
A drapery of dreams, I can't wait.
Each stitch a hope, woven just right,
In this garden of fabric, I take flight.

Tiny pockets for secrets, yes,
Sewing seeds, I'm feeling blessed.
Bright patterns sprout like weeds in spring,
Oh the joy that crafting can bring!

Every snip and rip comes with a grin,
An artful mess, let the fun begin!
Slicing fabric, it feels so fine,
This playful patchwork is truly divine.

In every layer, a giggle hides,
With quirky patches as my guides.
A tale of whimsy sewn with flair,
In this softly stitched love affair.

Twined in Temptation

A tapestry of wishes, all entwined,
Stitched in laughter, oh so kind.
Each thread a story, spinning round,
In tangled dreams, joy is found.

I laugh at choices, oh what a spree!
Glancing at what could never be.
My frolicsome fabric dances high,
As I craft with a mischievous sigh.

From polka dots to candy stripes,
Each whimsy piece ignites new types.
In crafty chat, we share a grin,
As silly stitches, we tuck within.

Bound by threads of giggle and cheer,
I'm sewing in moments, year by year.
In playful spirits, we won't retreat,
This fabric adventure cannot be beat!

Tapestry of Wishes

In a world of fabric dreams, they fly,
Stitched with laughter, reaching high.
Each thread a whim, each knot a joke,
As we dance around the fabric choke.

Colors clash in a playful twist,
Like socks and sandals—what a tryst!
Sewing mishaps, they make us squeal,
Life's a quilt, and that's the deal.

Patterned hopes dangle like charms,
In this crazy romp, nothing harms.
Grab a patch, let's make it right,
With snips and giggles, we'll take flight.

So unravel your wishes, dear friend,
In this tapestry, there's no end.
We'll craft our quirks with flair and glee,
A patchwork of joy, wild and free.

Adorned Aspirations

A funky brooch upon my coat,
Made of dreams that make me float.
A feather here, a sparkle there,
Accessorizing with utmost flair.

Each tiny trinket tells a tale,
Of silly hopes that never pale.
From mismatched earrings, oh what fun,
To wear aloofness like a pun.

Cameos and baubles jingle loud,
Join the dance, let's gather crowd!
With every clip and safety pin,
We'll rock the day and never thin.

So adorn your dreams, don't hold back,
In this circus, we're on track.
With laughter and flair, hearts take flight,
In this whimsical, radiant light.

Buttonholes of Emotion

In the garden where feelings sprout,
Buttonholes bloom, there's no doubt.
A wink here, a smile there,
Growing chuckles like fresh air.

Each color tells a juicy tale,
Of blushing hearts and comical fail.
Tug on feelings, see them sway,
A romance in the disarray.

The velvet whispers, oh, so sly,
Winking quietly, oh my, oh my!
Stitching quirks in every seam,
In this hilarity, we all beam.

So peek inside this playful patch,
Where laughter's the only match.
In buttonholes, emotions sprout,
With cuddles and laughs, there's no doubt.

Cords of Connection

Twisted threads that weave and tangle,
Pulling hearts in joyful wrangle.
With each tug, a giggle grows,
In this knot, hilarity flows.

Skipping ropes and playful ties,
A jumble of truth in disguise.
From fell swoops to comical lifts,
Oh, what fun this connection gifts!

Tugging on dreams, we laugh and spin,
With every twist, we reel you in.
From jolly loops to funky bends,
In this show, the joy transcends.

So let's connect and share the cheer,
With cords of laughter, nothing to fear.
In this silly dance of intertwine,
We'll bloom together, oh how divine!

The Drawstring of Elusive Love

In a world where socks just roam,
Tangled threads find their home.
With a drawstring that holds our dreams,
And laughter bursts at the seams.

Elastic (oh, how it stretches),
To accommodate love's wretched sketches.
But sometimes it snaps, oh dear,
Leaving us clinging to a beer.

Whiskers twirl like dancing mice,
In a game that feels quite nice.
Tie me tight or let me go,
Like this yo-yo, flows to and fro.

So here's to the strings that bind us tight,
And the laughter that tickles, oh what a sight!
For when we pull, and when we tease,
Elusive love brings us to our knees.

Palette of Pulsing Hearts

With a brush dipped in silly dreams,
We paint the skies in color schemes.
Hearts beat in outrageous hues,
As we skip around in mismatched shoes.

Crimson reds and bright mint greens,
Juggling feelings like circus scenes.
Tickled pink and feeling blue,
Who knew hearts could be so askew?

Winks and giggles in every stroke,
Artistic love, a whimsical joke.
So grab your palette and raise a cheer,
Let's splash some laughter, my dear!

Each heartbeat, a splash of comedy,
As we dance to our own melody.
In this mural, so abstract and free,
Love finds us all, it's plain to see.

The Singularity of a Heart's Need

In the realm of quirky desires,
We navigate like clowns on wires.
Each heartbeat a boisterous giggle,
With cravings that make us wiggle.

A singular need, so absurd and bright,
Like chasing fireflies in the night.
We hunt for snacks and dashing looks,
But end up lost in silly books.

With whispers of pizza and aims for romance,
We waltz through life in a wiggly dance.
A yearning that's both funny and grand,
With popcorn drizzled by fate's own hand.

So let's embrace this comical quest,
In the nexus of giggles, we're truly blessed.
For what we seek is simply this,
The laughter that fills a heart's wild bliss.

Wings of Fluttering Passions

With wings of laughter, we take to flight,
Chasing whims from day to night.
Fluttering hearts in a silly spree,
It's a carnival of joy, just you and me.

Around we twirl like confused butterflies,
Whispering secrets under starry skies.
Each flap a giggle, each turn a tease,
In love's playful winds, we flurry with ease.

Our passions soar in whimsical arcs,
As we dance like wild, bright sparks.
No serious faces, just pure delight,
For love's best moments are fleeting and light.

So join this flight of fluttering smiles,
As we frolic together across endless miles.
With silly joy and carefree cheer,
Our wings of passion will always steer.

Clasped Fantasies

In the drawer, they twinkle brightly,
Each a treasure, oh so sprightly.
They dance and play, a lively crew,
Stitching together dreams anew.

But wait, what's this? A button's grin?
It winks at me, oh where to begin?
Shiny and round, just calling my name,
In this fashion game, there's no shame!

Sew me a tale of laughs and cheer,
With a twist of fate, and a dash of beer.
Crafting a jacket of burst and flair,
With every clasp, I lose my care.

Oh, to be wrapped in whimsy's thread,
With silly ideas dancing in my head.
These clasped fantasies, such a delight,
Bring joyful giggles all through the night.

Fabric of Temptation

Woven in colors, bright and tight,
Temptations lurk in the fabric's light.
Each thread whispers secrets, oh what a tease,
Stitching up laughter with effortless ease.

A gathering of colors, bold and grand,
Holding dreams friendly, like a band.
Patterns dance, they tickle my skin,
In this playful realm, let the fun begin!

With every tug, anticipation grows,
As quirky patterns begin to expose.
A patch of joy, or a splash of zest,
This fabric calls, it knows what's best.

So I wrap myself in a world so wild,
Where even fabric wants to be styled.
Silly temptations, I can't resist,
With every moment, I laugh and twist.

Unraveling Hopes

In a basket piled high, hopes intertwined,
Unraveling threads, oh, what will I find?
A tangle of laughter, a knot of dreams,
Oops! There goes another, bursting at the seams.

Each snip and snarl, a giggle or two,
Hopes unraveled with a comedic view.
Pulling at strings with whimsical flair,
My heart dances free, floating in the air!

Yarns of joy lay scattered around,
In this messy chaos, my heart is found.
Unraveling hopes just leads to the fun,
With every new twist, a new day begun.

So bring on the laughter, the joy, the jest,
In a world of colors, my heart finds rest.
Unraveling whims, like confetti in flight,
Each moment's a treasure, sparkly and bright.

Pinning My Dreams

On a board of wishes, I pin them with glee,
Each little thought, a sprinkle of spree.
Colors and shapes, they giggle and sway,
While playful dreams come out to play.

With every pin, a story unfolds,
Nuts and bolts, and sparkly gold.
I chuckle so sweetly, as visions take flight,
In this whimsical land, everything feels right.

A patchwork of moments, sewn just for fun,
With every quirky pin, a new laugh begun.
Pinning my dreams like a butterfly's kiss,
In the fabric of life, I find silly bliss.

So here's to my board, where all hopes collide,
With laughter and joy forever allied.
In this playful realm where fun seems to gleam,
I'm forever pinning my outrageous dream.

Mending Broken Desires

Once lost a button, oh what a blunder,
Searched my pockets, found only thunder.
Stitched on a jelly, thought it would do,
My shirt looked tasty, how about you?

Tried adding ribbons, sequins, and lace,
Fashion disaster, but at least I'm in space.
My friends all laughed, I just wore a grin,
Claimed it was fashion, let the fun begin!

Needles and thread, a comedic scene,
Every stitch made me feel quite keen.
Who knew that mending could spark such delight?
At least my outfit gave them a fright!

In the end, I wore my silly pride,
With mismatched colors, I'm a joyride.
So here's to laughter, let the threads fly,
Life's a patchwork, just give it a try!

Threads of Longing

Sewed together dreams with glittering threads,
Lost one in the washing, there go my plans!
Pulled at the seam, and the fabric gave way,
Turns out my longing loves to play.

A mismatch of colors, a riot of hues,
My outfit looks like it drank too much booze.
Every thread frayed, a tale to unfold,
My heart laughs loud, and my laughter's bold!

Weave in some sparkles, a dash of flair,
Who knew my desires could start a fair?
Fabric shenanigans twirling around,
In this comical dance, great joy is found.

Embrace the chaos, stitch by stitch,
Life's just a quilt, full of humor and glitch.
With threads of longing, let's swing and sway,
In the world of fabric, we dance all day!

The Fastenings of Yearning

Fastened my hopes with a rusty old pin,
Tried to hold tight, but it kept giving in.
Fashioned a clasp from a candy bow,
Oh what a sight! Oh no, here we go!

My shirt went flying, oh what a show,
Caught in a breeze, it stole the whole show!
Every gust of wind, a giggle did bring,
I danced with the fabric, oh how we sing!

Pockets of wishes, tucked deep inside,
Fastenings swayed like a carnival ride.
A wobbly moment, my dreams took a spill,
But laughter won out, and it gave me a thrill.

So here's to the fastenings that make us whole,
With every surprise, we can still play our role.
Let's laugh at the fabric, our yearnings in tow,
In this jester's ball, let our spirits glow!

Clasped by Dreams

Clasped with a grin, in a wild little dance,
My dreams are absurd, but I'll take a chance.
Wore mismatched buttons, oh what a mess,
But who cares when laughter is my best dress?

Every twirl whispers a giggle or cheer,
My clothing's a riot, but my heart's full of cheer.
Sewed on some wishes beneath twinkling stars,
And held tight my hopes with some candy bars.

A crazy concoction of patterns collide,
In this fabric story, there's nothing to hide.
So let's clasp our dreams, with style that's bold,
In this jumbled fashion, let our tales be told.

With threads and stitches, we'll sum up our fun,
In the world of whimsy, I'm never outdone.
So clasped by laughter, let's frolic and play,
In this joyful fabric, we find our own way!

Hidden Stitches

In a drawer filled with odds and ends,
A treasure of threads and hidden bends.
Each tug a giggle, each pull a tease,
Crafting chaos with the greatest of ease.

With fabric whispers and spools in flight,
I stitch a tale that's sheer delight.
A needle's dance, a tailor's glee,
Sewing together my whimsy spree.

When threads unravel like a funny joke,
And pins tip over, oh what a poke!
Fuzzy socks meet a fancy shirt,
In the patchwork of life, we all get hurt.

So here's to the stitches, both seen and not,
In every mishap, joy's tightly caught.
A slip, a twist, then a chuckle anew,
Hidden stitches — life's playful glue.

The Ties That Bind

In mismatched socks, I find my flair,
The ties that bind us hang in the air.
They dance in the breeze, they wiggle and sway,
Creating mayhem in a humorous way.

A belt that's too tight, a tie with a fray,
Each moment a mess, yet brightens the day.
With laughter and stitching, what mischief unfolds,
Ties of affection in stories retold.

I trip on the laces, then I tie them again,
Each knot a reminder, where laughter has been.
With colors so wild and patterns askew,
The ties that bind us bring joy, it's true.

So here's to the moments when all goes awry,
In the fabric of friendships, we'll always comply.
With stitches and threads that create our live's vine,
It's the quirky little ties that delightfully shine.

Laced with Passion

Laces untied, like love on display,
Each slip of the knot means I'm here to play.
In a whirlwind of colors, we twirl and we spin,
Silly little jests make the moment begin.

With bows that won't hold and frayed ends,
A comedy's chaos where laughter transcends.
Step on my shoelace, I'll giggle not fume,
For it's the way we dance in this stitched-up room.

The shoemaker's joy and the cobbler's delight,
We'll tie up our tales in the soft evening light.
With passion in every uneven seam,
Life's a stage and we're part of the dream.

So lace up your stories, embrace every woe,
On the runway of life, we'll put on a show.
In the tapestry woven of laughter and cheer,
It's the laced-up adventures that we hold dear.

Sewn in Silence

A needle slips quietly, whispers abound,
Stitching up secrets in a world profound.
Laughter it muffles beneath the fabric,
Crazy thoughts tangled, oh, it's quite tragic.

In corners of quiet, I gather my thread,
Each twist of the yarn fills my heart with bread.
A snip and a cut, yet the humor runs deep,
Sewn in the silence where laughter will leap.

When seams start to chatter, oh what a sight,
A joking assembly line, full of delight.
With a thimble as crown and buttons amiss,
I craft a charade that's pure comic bliss.

So let's cherish the laughter that stitches and blends,
In the art of the quiet, where silence transcends.
With each subtle seam, a giggle will rise,
Sewn in the silence, just look in our eyes.

Laced with Seduction

In a shop where laughter spills,
Greatly mismatched, oh what a thrill!
A shoelace that dances, a buckle that sings,
Each twist and turn, an adventure brings.

A hat that's too small but twice the fun,
Silly antics when the day's begun.
With every clasp and each little hook,
We navigate mischief like an open book.

Funky fabrics beneath the light,
Strange colors that are a pure delight.
With every wardrobe mishap, oh dear,
The fashion faux pas bring us cheer!

Tangled up in a fashion spree,
Giggling at the tranquility.
In the world of fabric, we pursue,
It's the laughter that suits us, not the hue!

The Zipper of Uncertainty

Caught in my coat, the zip won't budge,
Pushed and pulled just a bit too much.
Each attempt like a dance gone wrong,
The fabric laughs, it must be strong.

Outside the wind plays a cheeky tune,
I'm stuck here spinning like a raccoon.
Do I call for help or brave it alone?
This zipper's a mystery all on its own.

Every wiggle just adds more doubt,
A simple task, but what's it about?
Do I risk a tear or take a dive?
In the quirk of fashion, I am alive!

With laughter echoing through the night,
The struggle becomes a comical sight.
In zippers and whims, we take our flight,
Laughing together, it feels so right!

Threads that Connect Us

Tangled threads weave tales untold,
With stitches of laughter, bright and bold.
Each knot we tie, a friendship cast,
In this fabric of life, we surely last.

A needle in hand, we stitch away,
Creating memories day by day.
Through threads of whimsy, we draw near,
The fabric of hearts, stitched without fear.

Colors collide, patterns collide,
In this quilt of joy, we take pride.
Every seam a story, every fold a laugh,
In the patchwork of life, we find our path.

Together we gather with needle and thread,
Through laughter and love, we forge ahead.
In the fabric of life, we see the sign,
That these silly threads, they truly shine!

Clutch of Unconfessed Feelings

A clutch that holds secrets, oh what a sight,
Fumbled thoughts sparkle like stars at night.
Zip it up tight, don't let it slip,
In this purse of dreams, we take a dip.

What if I told you, or dare not say,
This bag of emotions, it's here to stay.
Each pocket a puzzle, a riddle to find,
In the clasp of my heart, I'm ever so blind.

With every little jingle, what do I dare?
A wallet of wishes, love laid bare.
Do I reach for courage, or let it be?
In the clutch of confusion, I'm still so free!

As we wander this path of wishes unspoken,
Laughing at love where the silence is golden.
In this clutch of feelings, oh what a mess,
Life's tangled moments are truly the best!

Encircled by Anticipation

In a drawer, they giggle and play,
Hiding feelings, in a colorful way.
A twist, a turn, a pull, a pop,
Will they hold on, or will they drop?

My shirt's a circus, each snap and clack,
Wishing for confidence, but I lack.
A jolt of laughter, that's our game,
Each button a secret, none quite the same.

Through twists of fate, we dance and shout,
Each click a promise of what's about.
With mischief in mind, we stride and sway,
Clad in chaos, we'll find our way.

So here we are, a troupe of cheer,
Adventurous fashion, never fear!
With every tug and playful tease,
We wear our hopes like summer's breeze.

Fasteners of Hope

Jackets that flap, what a wild sight,
With each fastening, we take flight!
A zipper's grin, a button's wink,
Who knew chic was a game of brink?

Old coats laugh at my trendy plight,
Clashing colors, oh what a fright!
Yet in this madness, I find my groove,
Each frock a chance to make a move.

Belt loops holding tales of cheer,
Each story stitched, loud and clear.
In fabric fortune, we stumble and weave,
Fashion's a puzzle, can you believe?

So here's to chaos, let's take a stand,
With each fastener, life's unplanned.
From loopy laughs to stylish grace,
We weave our dreams, we own this space.

Stitched Promises

Threaded laughter in seams divine,
Each loop a promise, each knot a sign.
Hems that dance, tales to unfold,
Fabrics whispering secrets bold.

With every stitch, a chuckle flows,
Worn dilemmas no one knows.
Vibrant colors refuse to hide,
In the patchwork of fun, we take pride.

Even shirts with mismatched sleeves,
Can weave a tale that one believes.
We wear our quirks, our flaws, our fights,
In whimsical stitches, we find our nights.

Sew many dreams in a playful twist,
Life's silly moments, how could we resist?
From fabric's charm to laughter's view,
Stitches remind us, we're never through.

Glimmers of Rash Decisions

In frothy hats and shoes askew,
We laugh at choices, bold and true.
Colors clash, patterns collide,
Each outfit a journey, a wild ride.

Dresses with tremors, ties that sway,
In fickle fashion, we find our way.
A brooch of laughter, pinned just right,
We twirl and spin, full of delight.

From mismatched socks to glittery ties,
Each glimpse of joy a sweet surprise.
Whimsical outfits, daring and bright,
Guiding us through the curious night.

So leap into fashion, take the dive,
In the seam of folly, we all thrive.
With every choice we sprout a grin,
Woven together, let the fun begin!

Entangled with Longing

In the drawer, they sit and wait,
A dance of color, a twist of fate.
They wink and giggle beneath the light,
Oh, what mischief in the night!

One's red, one's blue with a sassy flair,
Caught in the laundry, a tangled affair.
Who knew style could cause such a fuss?
A closet quarrel – what's that about us?

They crave a tango on a well-tailored sleeve,
Yet grow dusty while we weave.
"Pick me, pick me!" they seem to shout,
Yet here I am, still turning about.

In the end, they smile, they tease,
For longing's fun with little ease.
These playful gems, oh, what a sight,
Laughing together through day and night.

The Weave of Intrigue

A tale is spun with thread so small,
Stitching secrets, one and all.
Each twist a story, a laugh, a sigh,
What's the truth, oh my, oh my!

Behind every seam, a jest resides,
In the fabric where mischief hides.
Silly patterns in a mismatched guide,
It's all in good fun, let's enjoy the ride!

A pop of polka, a splash of lace,
Who'd think attire could cause such a race?
With every chuckle and twirl in place,
We weave together, an odd embrace.

So raise a laugh, with all this flair,
From closet treasures, we freely share.
In the weave of intrigue, let's find our song,
With each stitch, we'll dance along.

Cords of Hidden Passions

Tangled threads in a playful mess,
Whispers of love, I must confess.
Ties that bind yet stretch so far,
Sneaky dreams on worn-out spar.

One's a velvet, soft and bold,
Its stories shimmer, brightly told.
While cotton crinkles in sheer delight,
Making mischief into the night.

What do I do with these shades so bright?
Fashion disasters? Oh, what a sight!
Yet behind the fabric, a wink appears,
Woven whispers through laughter and tears.

These cords of passion cling to style,
Making us chuckle, if just for a while.
For in their twist, we all will see,
Fun's the real thread that sets us free.

The Pressing Edge of Want

An iron clash, a heated play,
Fabrics longing to seize the day.
With every press, a sultry curl,
Entangled hearts in a fabric whirl.

The iron sings with a sizzle and pop,
As these tensions rise, they never stop.
"Press me close!" they start to beg,
On the edge of longing, they dance and beg!

Curved hems gawk and seams demand,
It's a fashion fanfare, quite unplanned.
Yet in the midst of this bold romance,
All they want is a playful chance.

So here's to the fun and whimsical spree,
With a zany touch from you and me.
On the pressing edge of playful want,
We share the giggles, a feathery flaunt!

Caressed by Warmth

In a coat made of laughs, I stroll,
Dancing through puddles, heart and soul.
A cat in a hat, oh what a sight,
Bumping into joy, it feels so right.

With cupcakes in pockets, I take a leap,
Ticklish butterflies, no time for sleep.
Each giggle a puzzle, not quite complete,
Chasing my shadow, we meet and greet.

The sun winks at me, a cheeky tease,
Breezes that play hide and seek with ease.
In this playful dance, I twirl and spin,
Living for moments that make me grin.

A marshmallow world, sweet and absurd,
Antics make laughter, oh how it stirred.
In a realm where delight finds its way,
I'll wear my joy like a sunny bouquet.

Patterns of Chasing Shadows

The sun plays tricks, stretching my form,
Underneath trees, I follow the norm.
Checkered my path, zigzagging delight,
Laughter in patterns, from morning till night.

Knocking on doors that lead to small dreams,
Whimsical wishes tucked in sunbeams.
With every step, a secret unfolds,
Dancing with shadows, the brave and the bold.

Twirling in circles, I stumble, I play,
My shadow's a partner, in a goofy ballet.
A mix of mischief, giggles collide,
In this realm of joy, there's nowhere to hide.

Pies in the sky, and clouds made of cream,
Life's a cartoon, more silly than dream.
Chasing the sunset, I laugh on the go,
Patterns of giggles, stealing the show.

The Loom of Unconfessed Want

In a closet of wishes, I weave and I spin,
Tangled in antics, I chuckle within.
A whimsical cloak cloaks my timid heart,
In a dance of the silly, I play my part.

With quirks and a zest for mischief's sweet song,
I find the absurd, where I feel I belong.
Like candy in pockets and bubbles that burst,
These fluttering whims leave me joyfully cursed.

A riddle of what could be tickles my mind,
In each secret hope, a joy I must find.
Whispers of laughter, the fabric of dreams,
In threads of the quirky, nothing's as it seems.

Stitching together my hopes oh so bright,
I craft my desires in colors of light.
The loom spins wildly, with giggles in hand,
Weaving a tapestry, silly and grand.

Ripples of Embrace

In a puddle of laughter, I skip and I glide,
Riding the ripples of joy by my side.
A splash of delight in a world made of glee,
I hug the horizon, where worries can't be.

With rainbows to chase and daisies to sing,
Ticklish adventures in each little fling.
I tumble and roll through the greenfields of cheer,
Each giggle a treasure, my heart's souvenir.

Soft whispers of breezes, the sunshine's warm glow,
Tickling my spirit, making it grow.
I embrace the silly, let worries all melt,
In a world of pure joy, I find what I felt.

As ripples dance lightly on shimmering streams,
I gather the moments that sparkle like dreams.
With hearts intertwined, let laughter unfurl,
In a whirl of delight, I twirl and I whirl.

Hems of Hope

In pockets deep, a hidden dream,
A button pops with a loud seam.
Laughter echoes, threads unwind,
Hope hangs loose, but we don't mind.

With needle's dance and snip of scissor,
A tailor's tape becomes a wizard.
Hems that flaunt a playful wit,
In fashion's game, we refuse to quit.

The seamstress winks, it's all a jest,
Stitching comedy, we're truly blessed.
Each tuck and fold a chance to play,
A hem of hope, come what may.

So gather 'round with thread and cheer,
For every flaw, let laughter steer.
With joy we craft our styles anew,
Sew silly dreams in shades of blue.

The Lure of Knotted Threads

In tangled yarns our tales are spun,
A playful twist, we laugh and run.
The lure of knots, a funny lot,
Each snarl a story, believe it or not.

Threads of chaos in every hue,
Tangled up in things we do.
With giggles shared and stitches crossed,
What was once lost is now embossed.

With every knot, a fable blooms,
Crafting laughter among the glooms.
We tie our tales with silly flair,
Knotted threads beyond compare.

So come unwind and join the fun,
Where unraveling leads to a pun.
In tangle's grip, we find our laughs,
In knots of joy, we are the crafts.

Clinging to Whispers

Whispers cling like threads on skin,
Half-stitched secrets tease our chin.
A giggle here, a blush or two,
In softest tones, we weave the brew.

Like fabric sways on windy days,
Our chatter dances in silly ways.
Clinging whispers, a secret lift,
Where every giggle is a little gift.

Hearts flutter 'neath the seams of talk,
In laughter's realm, we take a walk.
Clinging to joy, we spin our dreams,
In whispered tales like moonlit beams.

So come and share a laugh or two,
In the tapestry where friendships grew.
With whispers soft and grins so wide,
In every stitch, let love abide.

Hooks of Passion

Hooks of passion, where laughter lies,
In every poke, surprise complies.
A quirky dance with each tug and pull,
Oh, how these hooks get delightful!

With stitches bright, we play the part,
Creating joy, a crafty art.
Hooks that tease and hearts that jest,
In playful banter, we find our rest.

Each catch a giggle, a playful tease,
With hooks of fun, our worries cease.
A tapestry woven, our stories blend,
In every loop, there's love to send.

So twirl and spin, let's take the bait,
With laughter's grip, we celebrate.
Hooks of passion, what a stupor,
In jests and giggles, we find our trooper.

The Closure of Unspoken Words

In a drawer filled with secrets, they hide,
A tapestry woven, emotions collide.
With every missed chance, the tension grows,
Like soggy cereal, that's how it goes.

Lips sealed tight and laughter suppressed,
With language of silence, we jest and jest.
What if we shouted, let loose all those quirks?
Would it be chaos, or just more smirks?

When humor's a shield for what should be said,
We dance in this limbo, our feelings misled.
A giggle or chuckle, it's all just play,
In this game of heart, hey, who's in the fray?

Oh, the joy of ambiguity wrapped in a grin,
Each chuckle a chance, a gamble to win.
From whispers to roars, oh, what a delight,
In this comic ballet, we laugh into the night.

Ties that Bind

Two strings entwined, not quite a knot,
Our friendship's a circus—wild, but why not?
Like mismatched socks on a laundry day,
In this quirky quilt, we laugh and play.

From inside jokes to jumbled lines,
With tangled thoughts that dance like vines.
Who knew that chaos could be such fun?
Just wait till the day we both come undone!

As ribbons and bows create a show,
In the gift of our laughter, we ebb and flow.
Okay, it might be a little absurd,
But who needs logic when laughter's the word?

So let's twirl and trip down this whimsied lane,
Where shenanigans blossom despite any pain.
With ties that can tangle, and laughter that binds,
In this frolic of folly, our joy unwinds.

Pleats of Affection

Like a wrinkled shirt fresh off the line,
Our love's a fashion statement, oh-so-fine.
With pleats of affection, we strut our stuff,
In this catwalk of life, we can never get enough.

Fabric of friendship, stitched with a grin,
In this closet of chaos, we twirl and spin.
Those moments of joy, a fleeting parade,
With each delightful mishap, new memories made.

From crumpled notes to accidental slips,
Each wrinkle tells stories of friendship's trips.
A dash of sarcasm, a sprinkle of charm,
In our wardrobe of whims, there's never a harm.

So let's flaunt our quirks, like a dress on a rack,
In pleats of affection, we never look back.
With fabrics of laughter, we weave our own tale,
In stitches of joy, we cheerfully sail.

Toying with Temptation

Like a cat with a yarn ball, we play and tease,
With each twist of fate, we're brought to our knees.
The thrill of the chase, where laughter aligns,
In this playful dance, our whimsy defines.

At the corner of chaos, we spark and ignite,
Temptation's a game, we're in for the ride.
With winks and smirks, the plot thickens fast,
In this carnival of giggles, let's make it a blast.

Oh, the joy of the chase, it's all in good fun,
We leap and we bound, oh isn't it a run?
With whispers of mischief, we flirt with the edge,
Even as we play with the line of the ledge.

So here's to our banter, our playful spree,
In this teasing tango, you and me.
With moods lifted high, we frolic like children,
In this zany world, let's never stop building!

Creased with Lure

In a drawer of whimsy sat a charm,
A wrinkled smile that worked like a balm.
Each crease held secrets of playful delight,
Keeping hearts racing all through the night.

A twist of fabric, a cheeky plot,
With each little tug, another giggle caught.
Oh, the shenanigans they craft with a grin,
Stitching together what's lost and what's been.

I caught my reflection in a shiny red clip,
It winked and whispered, "Come, take a trip!"
To places where laughter rang loud and clear,
And joy was as abundant as chocolate beer!

So gather your colors, let's play this game,
Create little wonders, oh, let's go insane!
For in every fold, there's a tale to spin,
Who knew such mischief could start from a pin?

The Invisible Thread

Tangled in chaos, a soft little string,
It danced through the air with whimsical zing.
A pull here, a tug there, a giggle so bright,
Connecting us all in a comical flight.

A haphazard patch, like a cat in a hat,
With patterns and colors that looked like a spat.
But when you look closer, you'll find the plot,
It's stitched with laughter, waving forgot!

Through the fabric of folly, we weave and we splay,
Creating connections in our strange little way.
When one pulls a thread, the whole world can sway,
With chuckles and snorts that just make our day.

So here's to the threads that bind us with joy,
In the tapestry of life, there's no need to coy.
Let's wrap this round laughter, ignite the ignite,
And watch as our worries take flight in the night!

Creations of the Heart

A patchwork of dreams in a curious heart,
Sews moments with flair, a whimsical art.
Each pattern a giggle, each color a cheer,
Filling the fabric with warmth, oh, my dear!

With stitches of sunlight and threads of the moon,
We craft our adventures, and oh, how they swoon!
Each creation a story, a laugh, or a sigh,
Where joy's an abundance that floats up to the sky.

My apron's a canvas where nonsense can play,
With pockets of silliness tucked in for the day.
I'll bake up some laughter and serve it with glee,
For the heart finds its treasures when foolish and free!

So let's whip up a tempest in colors so bright,
With chuckles and giggles that dance in the light.
For creations of joy are the best kinds of art,
And laughter's the magic that fills every heart!

Dressed in Ambivalence

I wore a shirt that rubbed me wrong,
With patterns that seemed to sing a song.
Should I tuck it in, or let it flow?
The dance of choices puts on quite a show.

My pants are tight, my belt's a joke,
Each time I bend, I fear they'll choke.
What color's this? It's hard to tell,
My wardrobe's a circus, oh, what the hell!

Should I match my sock with my shoes of blue?
Or wear polka dots with my plaid? Who knew?
With mismatched flair, I strut with glee,
The fashion police won't capture me!

Each outfit's a riddle, a puzzling spree,
In the end, it's all just fabric free.
So laugh with me, let's have some fun,
Life is too short – it's time to run!

The Carefree Stitch

With a needle and thread, oh what a thrill,
I stitched my shirt, but it gave me a chill.
One seam too tight, and the button's a flop,
A dance with disaster, a fashion misstep!

My grandma warned me of scissors and seams,
But I ignored her, lost in my dreams.
Now thread pops out like confetti in June,
Every time I wear it, a laugh's in tune!

A patch on my elbow, a smile on my face,
Clothespins and patches create quite a place.
Handmade chaos, is this a trend?
Or just a comedy that won't see an end?

I gather my friends, in attire so bright,
Misfits of fabric, a colorful sight.
Together we rumble in laughter and cheer,
For in every mistake, there's joy that's sincere!

Entwinement of the Soul

You wore the hat, I had the shoes,
A rendezvous took us on a cruise.
Twisted yarn around our hearts,
In this tangled web, no one departs!

I pulled on your scarf, it was quite a catch,
You laughed so loud, I thought you'd hatch.
With mismatched charm, we share a grin,
Two threads in life, where do we begin?

We twirl in circles, our patterns collide,
With every slip, a giggle we hide.
In this fabric of moments, we find our sway,
Frayed edges dancing, come what may!

So here's to the stitches that hold us tight,
In this quirky quilt, we'll share our light.
For love's a blanket, stitched with a laugh,
In this patchwork of joy, we craft our path!

Stitches in Time

They say that time flies, but wear it well,
With stitches of laughter, we craft our spell.
A button popped off, it hit the floor,
Like a shooting star, it opened a door!

We gather the pieces, let's make a show,
Sew buttons on hats, let creativity flow.
A pet cat appears, with thread in its paw,
A feline designer? Oh, what a faux pas!

Irony's fabric works wonders at night,
We sew up our dreams, oh what a sight!
Stitching our futures, we giggle and sway,
With threads of delight, we brighten our day.

So here's to the stitches, the threads so divine,
In this whirlwind of fabric, together we shine.
Crafted with care, and a sprinkle of cheer,
In the tapestry of laughter, we'll always draw near!

Threads of Longing

In a drawer of chaos, they lay,
Each a promise of play and sway,
Concealing worlds where fantasies dance,
All stitched together in a threadbare trance.

A red one giggles, a green one sighs,
As denim dreams start to improvise,
Each grab a giggle, a crafty delight,
Who knew such charm hid out of sight?

The blue one whispers a joke so sly,
While the yellow's lost in a fashion high,
In the realm of fabric, they jest and tease,
Making memories like a summer breeze.

So gather them close, this button brigade,
In their woven wonder, laughter is made,
With every tug, a smile unfurls,
In stitches of joy, the silliness swirls.

Fastened Secrets

A clinking sound, what do I hear?
Oh just my secrets, don't you fear,
They're fastened tight with threads of glee,
In the pocket of my pants, you'll see!

The purple one claims, 'I hold the tales',
Of awkward moments and goofy fails,
While the shiny one loves to boast,
About the times I danced the most!

The others chime in, sharing their lore,
Of mischief done and socks they wore,
Stitched together in this quirky crew,
Fastened secrets that are oh-so-true!

When the needle slips and laughter flows,
Threads unwind, oh, how it goes,
In the recess of garments, a raucous delight,
These fastened secrets bring cheer at night.

Whispers in the Fabric

Whispers float from seams and threads,
Ticklish tales of what life spreads,
In the fabric's depth, a chortle resides,
As stitches giggle and laughter glides.

The plaid pants hum a cheerful tune,
While polka dots dance to the silver moon,
Their conversations weave a tapestry bright,
Of ridiculous moments, a comical sight.

Each fabric fold, a secret spun,
With cotton dreams sporting loads of fun,
As seams embrace, the stories mix,
Creating chaos, a fabric fix!

So listen close to the fabric's yarn,
For it's never just threads that keep us warm,
In this playful quilt of mirth, we find,
A patchwork of joy, intertwined.

Stitched Yearnings

In the cupboard lies a tapestry bold,
With stitched yearnings and stories untold,
Each color a jest, each pattern a laugh,
In a wacky world where we stitch our path.

A patch of turquoise claims it's the best,
While the frayed edges insist they're blessed,
Old buttons nod with their wise, sly glee,
Secret keepers of stitching esprit.

With fabric swirls and a thimble's grin,
The seams come alive where we all begin,
As laughter lingers in every thread,
Stitched yearnings dance, where no fears tread.

So let's embrace this fabric parade,
With stitches of giggles, we're never dismayed,
In this lively patch, let our dreams aspire,
For in sewn-up laughter, we'll never tire!

Unearthed Invitations

A note on the fridge, a magnet's proud hold,
A secret revealed, as stories unfold.
Like squirrels in winter, we hoard and we stash,
Digging through drawers for a vintage mustache.

With left shoes on right, and mismatched, no doubt,
An invitation's sent to dance and to shout.
Each errant sock whispers tales from the past,
Life's awkward waltz, oh how long will it last?

The fridge hums along, a soft serenade,
To moments gone by, in a comical parade.
As laughter erupts over popcorn on floor,
Let's toast to the chaos, who could ask for more?

So here's to our hearts, like jellybeans bright,
Sweet, tart, and misplaced; a chaotic delight!
With every mad moment, our spirits conspire,
Reviving the spark in this wonderful fire.

Embellishments of Desire

A hat on the cat, with a bow just so neat,
Strutting like royalty, a furball elite.
Scarves braided wildly, with colors so loud,
Fashion statements made, daring all to be proud.

In kitchens of chaos, where aprons collide,
A feast for the eyes, don't tell but don't hide!
With glittery spoons and plates piled high,
We dine like the jesters, oh me, oh my!

Ties tossed like confetti in air filled with cheer,
Every wrong choice feels perfectly clear.
We twirl and we laugh with uncontrolled glee,
For life is a stage, and we, the marquee!

So hang up your quirks, let them shimmer and shine,
Adorn every moment, make each one divine.
With friends by your side, life's whims are our grace,
In this dreamy bazaar, let's dance, let's embrace!

Tangles of Admiration

Like yarn in a closet, tangled and bright,
Our feelings arise, in a comical flight.
With compliments tossed, and laughter that swells,
Admiration is mixed with a sprinkle of spells.

A garland of giggles, with wink and a nod,
Each twist and each turn, a friendship unshod.
Pet names that trip on the tongue bring delight,
As we advocate hugs in our soft-hearted fight.

T-shirts of humor, designs far afield,
Worn proudly for all, no frowning concealed.
A dance-off at dusk, we shake off the night,
With missteps and goofs, it feels just so right!

So toast to the laughs, in our tangled embrace,
With every adventure, we carve out our space.
Through clumsiness seen, and the joy that we find,
Let hearts become full, with laughter entwined!

Cravings in the Fabric

In a quilt made of quirks, where colors collide,
Patchworks of joy and chaos, we hide.
A craving for patterns, for stories to weave,
Each stitch tells a tale, who could dare leave?

The buttons are dancing, like bees in the sun,
While threads twist and wiggle, it's all just good fun.
With intentions so fluffy, like clouds overhead,
Textures that tingle, where laughter's widespread.

Fabrics of friendship, each moment we sew,
From felting to folding, oh how we do glow!
With secrets entwined in our fabulous thread,
We savor the joy of the paths that we tread.

So wrap up the stories, let giggles prevail,
With bold prints and hues, we chart out our trail.
For life's a grand pattern, with colors so bright,
In this fabric of fun, we find pure delight!

www.ingramcontent.com/pod-product-compliance
Lightning Source LLC
Chambersburg PA
CBHW071126130526
44590CB00056B/2546